The Tub That Became a Boat

Story by Janie Spaht Gill, Ph.D.
Illustrations by Bob Reese

DOMINIE PRESS
Pearson Learning Group

Bobby filled the tub
to sail his sailboat.

2

3

The tub became a boat
and began to float.

It floated off the floor.

It floated out the door.

9

It floated down the stairs.

It floated between
some chairs.

It floated around the block.

It floated toward the dock.

Bobby shouted, "Whee!"

And he floated out to sea.

COAST GUARD

Curriculum Extension Activities

The Tub That Became a Boat

- Have the children draw a picture of a room in their house. Encourage them to choose a favorite thing they do in each room. Then have them write a sentence about each picture. If possible, have them select a beginning consonant sound that matches the beginning consonant sound of the room. For example, "I blow *bubbles* in the *bathroom*," or "I *play* on the *porch*."

- Have the children think of toys they play with in water. Have them draw and cut out pictures of them (or they can cut them out of a magazine). On a chart, paste and label all their pictures.

- Have a discussion with the children about the difference between reality and make-believe (nonfiction and fiction). Ask them if the events in this story could have really happened. Then ask them how the events in the story could be changed to make it a true story.

About the Author

Dr. Janie Spaht Gill brings twenty-five years of teaching experience to her books for young children. During her career thus far, she has taught at every grade level, from kindergarten through college. Gill has a Ph.D. in reading education, with a minor in creative writing. She is currently residing in Lafayette, Louisiana with her husband, Richard. Her fresh, humorous topics are inspired by the things her students say in the classroom. Gill was voted the 1999-2000 Louisiana Elementary Teacher of the Year for her outstanding work in primary education.

Softcover Edition ISBN 0-7685-2152-1
Library Bound Edition ISBN 0-7685-2460-1

Printed in Singapore
2 3 4 5 6 7 8 9 10   10 09 08 07 06 05

Dominie
Press

Pearson Learning Group

1-800-321-3106
www.pearsonlearning.com